Resilience-Centered Counseling

Resilience-Centered Counseling

A Practical Workbook

Caitlin Senk

Bassim Hamadeh, CEO and Publisher
Amy Smith, Senior Project Editor
Casey Hands, Production Editor
Jess Estrella, Senior Graphic Designer
Kylie Bartolome, Licensing Coordinator
Natalie Piccotti, Director of Marketing
Kassie Graves, Senior Vice President, Editorial
Jamie Giganti, Director of Academic Publishing

Cover image: Copyright © 2018 iStockphoto LP/pigphoto.
Design image: Copyright © 2018 iStockphoto LP/pigphoto.

Printed in the United States of America.

cognella® | ACADEMIC PUBLISHING
3970 Sorrento Valley Blvd., Ste. 500, San Diego, CA 92121

Contents

CHAPTER 7 .... **25**

POSTMODERNISM

Remembering Our Better Self 74

Strengthening Requires Sacrifice 75

Defining Strength 77

Mapping It Out Imagery Exploration: Student Reflections

Introduction

When I began to put this workbook together, I started to think about the concept of resilience and what this really means. My first foray into resilience research focused on the connection between resilience, the development of a substance use related disorder, and trauma. Within that process, I wondered how I was defining resilience and what part of my experience, values, and beliefs influenced that definition. Through a Western lens, resilience may be seen as more individualistic, rather than community driven or relational from a different cultural perspective. I continue to be curious about language and the construct of resilience. With that said, the *Resilience-Centered Counseling* text has one version of this concept, and it is important to acknowledge that it is just one perspective of how we might talk about and define resilience.

I also want to acknowledge my own intersectional privileges as a White, able-bodied, cis-woman and how some of the invitations listed in this workbook are informed by my intersectional identities. I acknowledge that these coidentities have helped enrich certain aspects of this project and perhaps resulted in some blind spots as well. However, I hope this workbook offers some insight and counselor self-awareness as you reflect on your own intersectionality and how those beautiful and complicated pieces of yourself show up in your relationships with your clients.

You will notice that the word "invitation" is used throughout this workbook, rather than language like "activity" or "exercise," to highlight the intentionality of accepting an invitation to process self. This workbook invites you to take moments of deep self-reflection and unpack your own process and ways of knowing. You may find at some point during these invitations that you come up with more questions than answers—that is just the point! This workbook is not intended to have "answers" to the ways in which you develop your resilient counselor identity, but rather provide an exploration that will continue to evolve.

I hope you are able to locate yourself and connect with some of these invitations throughout the workbook, while also allowing yourself to shift or adjust any aspect of the invitations to suit your own cultural needs and perspective. I underwent a significant growth process around humility and resilience during this project, and I invite you to find growth and resilience for yourself—whatever that looks like for you. This workbook is not intended to be a step-by-step process or guide to becoming a counselor, but instead a space to come back to, reflect, and process. My hope is that this workbook can function as a parallel process to your own counselor development and be helpful to your work with clients.

This workbook is intended to be a supplemental exploration of your personal and counselor identity in order to connect more deeply with the chapters of the *Resilience-Centered Counseling* text. The pages to follow will encourage verbal and written reflections, somatic invitations, and imagery exploration. The verbal/written reflections will invite you to engage in reflection with pen/paper or have a conversation with another individual. The somatic invitations will encourage you to engage in processing yourself holistically with your body. Finally, the imagery exploration will be an opportunity to use creative or artistic expression to process. Everyone processes information differently, and the options under each invitation provide choices based on the most helpful ways for you to learn. There may be moments to challenge yourself outside your comfort zone and others to ease in with invitations that feel more familiar. You will notice that most of the invitations focus on relational thinking and bringing together collective voices and perspectives.

I hope this workbook can be a starting point and open the door for more conversation around this idea of resilience and how it is manifested through different lenses. My email is caitlin@cmscounselingpgh.com and I would love to hear your insights, thoughts, or corrections. My goal is to continue to break down, expand, and grow this concept into one that encompasses many voices from different cultures.

COUNSELOR AS HEALER, CONSCIOUSNESS AND EMPIRICISM, SELF-HEALING

Sitting in Awareness

Intention

We have all sat in the space of self-deprecation and judgment. Self-doubt tracks each of us throughout the day and asks us to question our value in a variety of contexts and interactions. This is also true of the counselor, who may find themselves sitting across from their client, juggling a space of listening to two voices—the clients and their own.

As we try to listen to our clients, even with nonjudgment, we all too often find ourselves in an internal conversation, questioning our words, reflections, and ideas. You have likely been in this space, possibly even as you read this book.

Verbal Reflection

| Duration: 5 minutes | Materials Needed: None, Pen/Paper optional |

The first step is in simply sitting with our own voice, aware that it is there. Listening to it, yet not acting. "I wonder if I should have done _____" can shift to "I notice my doubt as I read." Nothing to do, just listen.

As you reflect on the readings in *Resilience-Centered Counseling*, listen to what comes up for you. Which of your own lived experiences arise as possible mirrors in bettering your own understanding of yourself? Then allow yourself the gift of nonjudgment and empathy.

There I am ... that is me ... and that is ok.

_____

_____

_____

_____

_____

Somatic Invitation

Duration: 5–10 minutes   Materials Needed: Pen/Paper

Orienting towards the physical body can be uncomfortable or triggering for many reasons, including but not limited to chronic pain, gender dysphoria, breathing difficulties, cardiovascular challenges, and/or trauma. Please move at your own pace with somatic explorations. You may also find it helpful to think of your body as a balloon or series of balloons that can inflate and deflate with breath if some distance between you and your physical experience is supportive.

Practice progressive muscle relaxation (Jacobson, 1938). If possible, invite yourself into a space where you are sitting comfortably upright with your back lengthened and supported or lying down. Focus on lengthening and deepening your breath by feeling the air go in through the nose and fill up the empty cavities in your body.

Once your inhalation and exhalation are balanced and smooth, tighten both of your fists, holding the tension for about 5 seconds, and then quickly relax for about 20 seconds. Follow this pattern with other body parts: forehead, jaw, shoulders, biceps, forearms, stomach, thighs, and toes. Concentrate on noticing your feelings and sense of relaxation throughout your body. Once finished, journal the experience and what awareness you were sitting with.

References

Jacobson, E. (1938). *Progressive relaxation* (2nd ed.). Chicago: University of Chicago Press.

Mindful Listening

Intention

Embodying empathy is a skill involved with being deeply within another's experience while also holding onto enough of yourself to stay grounded and present in the moment. This may create dissonance as you attempt to "help" in the counseling role and also challenge yourself to sit with a client's pain without acting.

Somatic Invitation

Duration: 5+ minutes	Materials Needed: None

On your own, find a comfortable place to sit or stand and spend a moment breathing as you normally would. Now begin breathing with intentionality by breathing in for 4 seconds, holding the breath for 7 seconds, and then exhaling for 8 seconds. Be mindful of the way your breath fills your body, and notice where the breath goes. Minds wander, so when this happens, notice where it goes and then refocus on breathing when you can.

Continue in this way for as long as you may need, with the goal of trying not to change the way your body is breathing, where your mind goes, or how you are feeling. Just let yourself be.

_____

_____

_____

_____

_____

_____

_____

Verbal Reflection

Duration: 10–20 minutes   Materials Needed: Partner

Think of a recent experience you had that brings up some mild feelings (sad, angry, hurt, confused, etc.). In a dyad, share this experience where each of you will have the opportunity to sit in the role of listener and storyteller. Plan to spend about 10 minutes in each role.

In the role of listener, how aware are you of the feelings enmeshed in the story? Notice and process if you are compelled to do something, like solve a problem or find the silver lining. Challenge yourself to be a mindful listener by allowing empathy to fill the space and your body without judgment and without trying to change the circumstances of your partner's story. After your partner has shared, spend a moment writing down your judgments, thoughts, habits, desires.

In addition, reflect on what feelings you noticed for your partner, their strengths, possible beliefs, and other struggles that may be present for them in an effort to continue accessing empathy.

Switch with your partner and share your reactions and what was surfacing around this exercise.

_____

_____

_____

_____

_____

_____

Throwing out the Toolbox

Intention

We gain a wealth of knowledge in counseling programs, including the history of theories along with their evidence-based techniques. We learn how to use basic and foundational counseling skills like summarizing, reflecting feelings, hunches, paraphrasing, etc. While those skills are important, sometimes they can take you away from the present moment and active listening and, instead, create internal noise that may question whether we are listening "correctly." Sometimes throwing out the toolbox creates space for moments of presence and deep listening without being in our own thoughts.

Verbal Reflection

Duration: 10–20 minutes	Materials Needed: Partner

In a dyad, practice staying present with a partner as they share a story with you for 5 to 10 minutes. This story can be about any experience (i.e., conflict, joy, sadness, frustration, excitement). It may be helpful to set a timer for 3-minute segments in which you notice thoughts in the first segment, followed by noticing feelings, and then noticing bodily sensations.

As the listener, what feelings come up for you as you think about letting go of theories and techniques in the moment? Sometimes this may feel uncomfortable. It is not about throwing these skills out the window, but instead about embodying them while also staying present with the person across from you.

Reflect on this experience with your partner before switching roles.

_____

_____

_____

_____

_____

Systemic and Relational Thinking

Intention

By influencing the inherent power of counselors to assess and orchestrate behavioral interventions, the need for developing empathic relationships and emphasizing the worldview and strengths of clients is diminished. Token economies are still widely used in inpatient settings, and with the pressure for mental health agencies to demonstrate empirically supported treatments (EST), clinicians are more likely to focus on manualized treatment protocols, rather than the inherent strengths of clients, or the healing nature of quality therapeutic relationships.

How might counselors move away from assumptions and diagnosing behaviors or symptoms to staying curious and focusing on systems and relational connections? Essentially, what can you do as a counselor to take yourself outside of token economies and lean into the relational pieces of a client's experience and the therapeutic relationship itself?

Verbal Reflection

Duration: 20–40 minutes   **Materials Needed: Partner**

In order to facilitate oneself to operate systemically while also connecting to the immediacy and multicultural aspects in the therapeutic relationship, we must unpack our assumptions to benefit both ourselves and our client. To do this, it is important to reflect on what these assumptions and biases are. Feel free to refer to the "Mapping It Out" exercise on page 54 to identify some assumptions that can manifest through your values and beliefs.

Think about a client/demographic that may be challenging for you to work with given your own assumptions and biases. It may be helpful to refer to the Ratts et al. (2015) Multicultural and Social Justice Counseling Competencies below when considering your dyad (i.e., privileged counselor–marginalized client; marginalized counselor–privileged client).

What judgments come to mind when you think about this particular client? How does your position or intersectionality contribute to your judgment and understanding of this client?

In a dyad, one person will act as the client while the other will play the role of clinician for 15 to 20 minutes. As the clinician, consider assumptions, biases, and judgments that came up for you. Consider what it would be like to hold your own values and beliefs, acknowledge them, and make space for your client's perspective as well. How might this shift the way you show up with your client?

_____

_____

_____

_____

_____

Somatic Invitation

| Duration: 5–10 minutes | Materials Needed: None |

Take a moment to get comfortable either seated or lying down. Close your eyes and begin focusing on your breath and bring awareness to a specific part of your body. Spend about 30 seconds noticing the sensations in this part of your body. After 30 seconds, release your focus and move to another part of your body and engage in the same sequence. When ready, release your focus and come back into your surroundings.

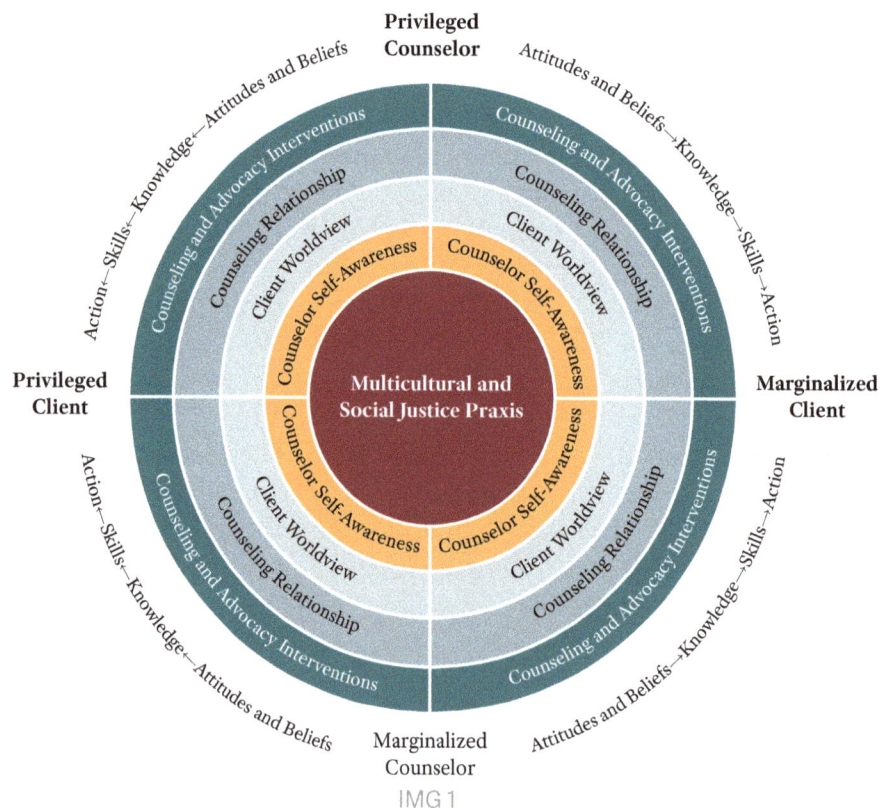

IMG 1

Spend some time reflecting on shifting away from personal values, beliefs, judgments, and biases toward a more client-centered perspective. Once again, engage in the same body scan as above and notice what may have shifted or changed in your inner physical or energetic experience.

_____

_____

_____

_____

_____

References

Ratts, M. J., Singh, A. A., Nassar-McMillian, S., Butler, S. K., McCullough, J. R. (2015). Multicultural and social justice counseling competencies. https://www.counseling.org/docs/default-source/competencies/multicultural-and-social-justice-counseling-competencies.pdf?sfvrsn=20

Image Credits

IMG 1: Source: https://www.counseling.org/docs/default-source/competencies/multicultural-and-social-justice-counseling-competencies.pdf?sfvrsn=20.

Experience of Anxiety and Meaning

Intention

In the human experience, no one is free from suffering. Life can challenge us in ways that we least expect, and in these moments, we find ourselves feeling ill prepared as if there is something we could have done or controlled to avoid the pain. Yet, when we think back on some of our deepest moments of growth and learning, they often emerge out of some of the harshest conditions. What empowers us to learn, upon hindsight, is rarely something that someone said or told us to think or feel. It is a reflection in the mirror, where, over time, we find ourselves stronger simply by surviving. That vantage we gain with time is actually a relationship within ourselves and likely the outcome of many conversations—internal with ourselves (conscious and subconscious) and external with others in our support network. When we seek to avoid painful experiences out of the natural instinct to survive, there is nothing wrong with us—we are being human. Yet, when courage meets that desire to avoid, we may find ourselves stronger than before. In this way, the existence of fear drives us to courage and to the choice to face challenges, to connect to ourselves and to reach out to others. When our clients find us, they are already on that path for themselves, and in our work, we should honor those first steps as the critical baseline of resilience.

Somatic Invitation

Duration: 5–10 minutes	Materials Needed: None

Take a moment to slow down and create awareness with your surroundings. Look around you and notice three things you can see, two things you can touch, and one thing you can hear. Name the qualities of these items and experiences with as much detail as you can (i.e., colors, shadows, textures). What did you notice happening to your body in this experience? Where did you notice your thoughts?

_____

_____

_____

_____

Written Reflection

Duration: 5–10 minutes   Materials Needed: Pen/Paper

Take a moment to think back on a time in your life where you faced a depth of hardship that scared you. A time where you felt so anxious that you didn't know what to do next, to think or to feel. Think back on how you took a breath, you took steps, and someone in your network witnessed your courage. They likely didn't climb the mountain for you, but in their witnessing of your climb, you gained the strength to keep going. They saw you, so you could also better see yourself. Reflect and journal on how being seen and in community can impact the way that you see yourself and your journey.

First Impressions of Mental Health

Intention

Where does your own thought begin and another's end? While philosophical in nature, this question also creates awareness around the importance of understanding our own values and belief systems. Processing the ways that we have learned about mental health is pivotal to understanding how we will show up in the counseling space.

Written Reflection

Duration: 5–10 minutes	Materials Needed: Pen/Paper

Recall your first impressions of psychology, counseling, and/or mental health, whether through personal experiences, media portrayal, or another interaction that you had with mental health, and reflect on the following:

- How does this currently inform your developing counselor identity?
- Which media portrayals of mental health have you struggled with or resonated with?
- How have you internalized underlying messages of mental health that may be harmful?
- How might this first impression have influenced your own desire to step into the mental health field?

_____

_____

_____

_____

_____

INTERDEPENDENCY, SECOND ORDER CHANGE, TRAUMA, AND RESILIENCE

1. OPENNESS TO CHANGE
2. UNIQUE OUTCOMES AND EFFORTS
3. CONNECTION WITH THE SELF
4. EXPERIENCING OPENNESS

Openness to Change

Intention

Being open is an important part of developing your counselor identity. This can mean being open to new ideas, ways of thinking, and worldviews, which all contribute to the way that we can show up with our clients. The invitations below allow space to reflect and challenge yourself around your current ability to be open and also perhaps uncover some limitations that may be beneficial for you to continue unpacking.

Somatic Invitation

Individual

Duration: 5–10 minutes	Materials Needed: None

Explore physical sensations of tension and release throughout the body. Start from the feet and move up through each part of the body creating tension and then releasing along the way and then go back down to the feet once you reach the head. End this process with exploring tension in the entire body followed by a release.

_____

_____

_____

_____

_____

_____

Dyad

Duration: 10–20 minutes   **Materials Needed: Partner**

Consensual learning acknowledgment: Prior to engaging, discuss your level of participation with options to skip an exercise if you are not able or comfortable. If you are using an online learning platform, also create the option to keep the camera on or off to increase accessibility.

Partner A slowly reads the following word groups while Partner B explores movement. Encourage the moving partner to explore sounds and vocalizations but to limit verbal processing. After about 5 minutes, switch roles.

After each turn, the moving partner (Partner B) has an opportunity to share what they experienced. As Partner B, reflect on noticing when your body felt opened and when it felt closed.

Witnessing partner (Partner A) has 1 minute to share what they experienced while watching. Emphasize personal reflections (i.e., When I saw your arms move from open to closed, I felt more space throughout my chest, a sense of mixed awe, sadness, and curiosity), rather than an evaluation, judgment, or interpretation of the other's movement (i.e., When I saw your arms move from open to closed, I knew/thought/wondered if you were expressing sadness about your recent loss).

Word Group A	Word Group B	Word Group C
Annoyed	Frustrated	Devastated
Insecure	Shaky	Powerless
Stuck	Stimulated	Understanding
Curious	Reflective	Kind
Eager	Animated	Spontaneous
Determined	Passionate	Whimsical

Verbal Reflection

Duration: 10–20 minutes	Materials Needed: Partner

With a partner, reflect on an experience where you were open to change. If needed, use the following questions to guide your process of engagement:

- What were the conditions of this experience?
- What allowed/supported you to change?
- How did you know you had to change or wanted to change?
- What allowed a movement toward change?
- Who/what community supported this change?
- How did you know you had shifted/changed?
- What physical/bodily sensations relate to being closed off to change versus being open to self-reflection, accountability, and movement toward action that is more greatly aligned with one's personal value system?

_____

_____

_____

_____

_____

_____

Imagery Exploration

Duration: 10–30 minutes	Materials Needed: Pen/Paper

Processing Impact of Change

Take a piece of paper and draw a line through the center. Utilize the left side to explore who you were before the shift/change and the right side to explore who you are afterward.

You could write adjectives, themes, beliefs, thoughts, or draw, use art, magazine cuttings, etc. to engage in this exploration.

Being Open and Closed to Change

Reflect on a time when you experienced change yourself. Reflect on a time when you were not open or able to change.

On the left side of a piece of paper, reflect on how it was to experience your own inability to change. On the right side, reflect on what it was like to experience change.

Noticing Change in Others

Reflect on a time when you experienced another person or system change. Reflect on a time when you experienced the inability of another person or system to change.

On the left side of a piece of paper, reflect on how it was to experience another's inability to change. On the right side, reflect on what it was like to experience another change.

Systemic Change

Reflect on a time when you were able to step forward to move a collective shift/change in a system (examples include relational, family, professional, academic, political, environmental, etc.).

Create three columns on a piece of paper. In the left column reflect on what it was like to step forward into change. In the middle column, write out what the outcome was. In the right column, write down what you learned from the experience.

OR

Left column: What was it like to see something that needed to be changed but not have the ability, willfulness, courage, resources, or privilege to advocate for change?
Middle column: What was it like to witness the injustice from a place of powerlessness?
Right column: What did you take away from that experience?

_____

_____

_____

_____

_____

_____

Unique Outcomes and Efforts

Intention

The questions below elicit *efforts* that highlight unseen strengths, introduce the idea that problems are not always occurring (exceptions), and provide a window into future "ways of being" (see textbox below). It further guides well-meaning counselors away from the temptation to judge or blame clients for their difficulties and encourages a mutual remembering of the better moments in a person's lived experience.

Remembering Unique Efforts

What is *different* about you in those moments when the struggle or concern has less of a hold on you?

_____

_____

_____

_____

What do you have more *access* to in yourself in moments that feel "more on track"? What is your best guess about how this happens for you?

_____

_____

_____

_____

_____

How do you keep the struggle or concern at bay when you *need to*? What are you more <u>focused</u> on during those times?

_____

_____

_____

_____

_____

As you come to terms with your current struggle, *who* is in your corner, and what might they whisper in your ear?

_____

_____

_____

_____

_____

(Adapted from White & Epston, 1990)

Even in the bleakest circumstances, we can glean resources, strengths, and exceptions to the problem pattern through a conversation of daily events where the smallest details can contradict perceptions of defeat and hopelessness.

Verbal/Written Reflection

Duration: 5–15 minutes   Materials Needed: Pen/Paper or Partner

With a learning partner, or individually with pen in hand, consider a current life struggle and reflect on the questions above. They are designed to remember those moments of resilient efforts that have been forgotten in the wake of your current struggle. Following each remembrance, be sure to push yourself with "and what else was different?"

_____

_____

_____

_____

_____

_____

References

White, M., & Epston, D. (1990). *Narrative means to therapeutic ends*. W. W. Norton & Company.

Connection with the Self

Intention

While we live in a world that is in a state of constant connection, sometimes we can feel disconnected from ourselves. The body does not exist in a vacuum separate from our mind. Taking the time to find this connection in a way that feels congruent with your experience of self can be an important part of connecting with clients.

Verbal/Written Reflection

Duration: 5–10 minutes   Materials Needed: Partner optional

Take a moment to consider times in life where you learned the most about yourself. Write these down in whatever way feels most comfortable to you (i.e., bullet points, sentence, story, etc.).

In a dyad, share with your partner some times that came to mind. As the listening partner, write down your own thoughts, feelings, and memories that emerge from what your partner is saying. What parts of their story are you feeling connected to? Are there aspects of their story that are difficult for you to understand from your own perspective? Is there a part of your own perspective that is getting in the way of connecting with your partner and their story?

_____

_____

_____

_____

_____

_____

Somatic Invitation

| Duration: 5–10 minutes | Materials Needed: None |

Find a space that feels comfortable to you. Working from the bottom up, identify spaces in your body that feel tense or constricted, as well as spaces that feel loose and relaxed. Notice what you are thinking and feeling about each of these spaces in your body. Is there a story you are telling yourself about these feelings? Are there stories that the body has or wants to tell? Is there a story your mind is telling about the body?

What are you noticing about the connection between your mind and body? Are there places of stronger and weaker connection?

Continue scanning your body with the intention of connection. If you are noticing some activation, take a moment to engage in the following diaphragmatic breathing:

Find a comfortable position to sit or lie down. Place one hand on your belly, just below your rib cage, and another on your chest to offer a guide to your breathing. You may also imagine a pair of additional hands on your upper and middle back. Think about going slowly and smoothing out your breath as it enters and exits your body, filling up your belly, chest, and back. Bring attention to the rhythm, and begin to deepen your breath by getting to the "top" of your exhalation before letting a full breath release as you exhale. Then, pause for a period of time that feels comfortable to you. Continue to inhale slowly and deeply and focus on your intention with breathing.

_____

_____

_____

_____

_____

Intention

These invitations are an opportunity to unpack some of the processing done in the previous reflections of openness and put them into practice. As counselors, we can spend a lot of time focusing on the process and fall short on actionable steps. Taking action and answering the "what now?" can be the most difficult and challenging aspect of change and openness.

Written Reflection

Duration: 5 minutes   Materials Needed: Pen/Paper

Research has demonstrated that the act of witnessing alone has extensive healing potential. If we as counselors are able to step into the experience of a client's story, rather than just the content or context of the story itself, we can create a containing that elicits self-soothing.

Think about a time when you told a story to someone and you felt like they really heard you and walked in the story alongside you. Reflect and write on the following ideas:

- How did you feel at that moment?
- Conversely, how do you feel when someone seems more concerned with the content of your story rather than your perspective of it?
- Take a moment to process what the difference is for you here and what you need in these situations.

Somatic Invitation

Duration: 5–10 minutes	Materials Needed: Partner

In dyads, have one person share an experience they had with conflict. This can be something that occurred at work, at home, or in any space.

While your partner is talking about their conflict, allow yourself to invite the affective-intensive experience into your inner world. Reflect on the physical sensations that may be present with you as you hold this experience within your body. What are you noticing about your body? Is there resistance or tension in holding your partner's experience? How is your body telling you that you are open? How might your body be communicating that it is closed?

_____

_____

_____

_____

_____

Imagery Exploration

Duration: 5–10 minutes	Materials Needed: Multimedia optional

Explore a moment when you were closed from change or openness. Using images, drawings, movement, or even vocal intonation, express what it was like for you to be closed.

Now, explore a moment when you were open. Using the same medium you chose above, express what it was like for you to be open.

Take some time to reflect on what your body or mind may be needing to shift from a closed to open position. What comes to mind? How might you engage in this shift today, even in microform? How do you know when you are being open? What about the way you perceive others as being open?

_____

_____

_____

_____

POSTMODERNISM

Inherent Wisdoms

Intention

The text promotes a liberating approach that invites people to take their power back from whatever trauma, biological fact, differently abled condition, or oppression they are experiencing or been exposed to.

Verbal Reflection

Duration: 5–10 minutes	Materials Needed: Partner

In dyads, have a shared conversation about the wisdom you hope to take from a current struggle or life event.

What do these wisdoms say about your deepest values? Which of these would you like to hold closer during the upcoming week?

REMINDER: As a listener, refrain from benevolent statements of privilege (e.g., "that's great," or "good for you"). Engage with checks of understanding only.

_____

_____

_____

_____

_____

Enriching Beliefs

Intention

Postmodern approaches do not posit real truths about the human experience. Comb's early theory on perception explained "… how a person behaves will be a direct outgrowth of the perceptions existing at any moment" (1954, p.65). These perceptions are constantly in a state of revision influenced by interaction with others, culture, and society at large. In other words, it is not so much an understanding of "multiple realities," as it is that our perception of ourselves and the world around us is unique, varied, and constantly being added to or revised. This perception is understood as a self-narrative: an internal conversation of who we are in relation to our surroundings at any given moment in time. It is how our beliefs of ourselves and our surroundings are developed.

Written Reflection

Duration: 5–10 minutes   Materials Needed: Pen/Paper

Postmodern approaches address oppressing self-narratives that diminish one's worth, through a mutual consideration of other possible life stories that might also be true. These invitations are designed to thicken or enrich one's beliefs with elements of agency and efficacy (e.g., *"I'm wondering if your fatigue might also reflect the weight of responsibility you carry for others?"*).

Take a moment to consider your own self-narrative and reflect/write on the following:

- What beliefs do you hold of yourself?
- How might you enrich these beliefs?
- Does your narrative offer agency and efficacy of self? If not, how might you wish to expand or shift what you believe about yourself and/or others?

_____

_____

_____

_____

_____

_____

References

Combs, A. W. (1954). Counseling as a learning process. *Journal of Counseling Psychology, 1*(1), 31–36.

Telling Stories: Invitations for Collaborative Change

Intention

Narrative Therapy (NT) is grounded in the existential idea that individuals are unique in how they relate to the experiences of their lives (Kierkegaard, 1954), as well as to the internal perception they have of themselves. If these internal perceptions become *problem saturated*, self-denigrating beliefs and emotional suffering can result. The intent of NT is to assist individuals and families with eliciting new aspects of their stories so that "unique outcomes" can be constructed as well as future perceptions of themselves and others (White, 1989).

Verbal Reflection

Duration: 5–15 minutes	Materials Needed: Partner

When a self-narrative is problem saturated, an individual, family, or even a system can enmesh their sense of self with their problems.

In a dyad, one person will share a story while the other person listens for the beliefs and narrative of the person sharing. As the listener, use the collaborative invitations below as a guide to being curious with your partner about their narrative, and challenge yourself and them to hold space for multiple perspectives or truths. Plan to spend about 5 minutes in each role.

As the person sharing your story, what was it like to hear these invitations? What did you notice about your self-narrative?

_____

_____

_____

_____

_____

Narrative Counseling

(Opening Space)

- What does the problem wish you to believe about yourself? What has influenced this belief (e.g., family, culture, socio/political)?

_____

_____

_____

_____

- What have these ideas of yourself robbed you of?

_____

_____

_____

_____

- How much of your life does it control? Are you OK with this? What is it like to say out loud?

_____

_____

_____

_____

- Do you think it is best for (the problem) to run your life, or would it be better to run your own life?

_____

_____

_____

_____

_____

- What do you imagine might be different about you if you took back even a small bit of your life?

_____

_____

_____

_____

_____

Imagery Exploration

Duration: 10 minutes   Materials Needed: Pen/Paper

Think about your own self-narrative and imagine each story line of problems or successes as a thread that crisscrosses one another.

Take a piece of paper and draw a line from left to right on the page for each story that you identified as a problem in your self-narrative. Then, draw a line from the top of the page to the bottom for each story that you identified as a success.

Consider this visual representation as a net of your experiences and emotions. What do you notice about the threads and the importance of their existence?

References

Kierkegaard, S. (1954). *Fear and trembling: and the sickness unto death*. Princeton University Press.

White, T. G. (1989). *Collected papers* (Vol. 1).

Accepting Exceptions: Invitations for Collaborative Change

Intention

At its core Solution-Focused Therapy (SFT) is collaborative, assuming that people and families have both the resources and capacity for change. As Eve Lipchik (2011) noted, "therapists don't change clients, clients change themselves" (p.7). She also cautioned against well-meaning counselors seeking to relieve clients of their pain, becoming too protective from their suffering rather than helping them use their own resources, strengths, and capabilities to take care of themselves.

Written Reflection

Duration: 10 minutes	Materials Needed: Pen/Paper

Consider the idea of being patient with yourself because we are always growing and shifting, which makes maintaining a regulated state nearly impossible as we find tolerance with the tension that is created from growth. The solution is connection made from the journey rather than getting from point A to B.

Think about a time when you were faced with a struggle, and consider the reflective questions below that focus on exceptions to problems in SFT. Take a moment to think about times when the struggle had less of a hold and perhaps what strengths you were able to tap into that opened up the door to something other than the problem or struggle.

_____

_____

_____

_____

_____

_____

Solution-Focused Therapy

(Exceptions)

- What is different about you when you are more able to keep your head above water? What is your guess on how you are able to do that at those times?

_____

_____

_____

_____

- What is different about those times when things are a bit more on track for you? What is your guess about how you are able to keep the problem at bay a bit better?

_____

_____

_____

_____

- When the problem is less present, what are you thinking about instead? What ideas and activities seem more available?

_____

_____

_____

_____

- What is your guess about what others might notice in you when the problem is less present?

_____

_____

_____

_____

_____

Imagery Exploration

Duration: 10–30 minutes   **Materials Needed: Multimedia**

Take a piece of paper and divide it into two sections by either drawing a line or folding it in half. Feel free to use what medium(s) you are drawn to (paper/pencil, painting/drawing, etc.) in order to depict two images, one for each section of the paper. One image should be a representation of yourself within a struggle or problem. The other image should be how you see yourself without the struggle or problem. Once finished, reflect on what surfaces for you around what you notice in these two images. How are they similar? How are they different?

_____

_____

_____

_____

_____

References

Lipchik, E. (2011). _Beyond technique in solution-focused therapy: working with emotions and the therapeutic relationship_ (Ser. The Guilford Family Therapy Series). Guilford Press.

CHAPTER 8

FEMINISM AND RESILIENCE

Resilience and the ADDRESSING Model

Intention

The model as presented below is culturally bound to white, Eurocentric culture, systems, and values. This may look different from other cultural and social identity locations. It is also crucial that we all consider the intersectionality of our identities.

Verbal Reflection

Duration: 10–20 minutes	Materials Needed: Partner, Pen/Paper

Consider with your dyad partner your own addressing model (agent) in comparison to the clients you work with (target). What is your reaction? In what ways might this inform your understanding of your clients and colleagues moving forward?

_____

_____

_____

_____

_____

Somatic Invitation

Duration: 10–15 minutes	Materials Needed: None

Take a moment with each identifier and think about embodying each identity. What do you notice about how these pieces live within your physical body? How much space or energy do they take up? How might you notice when one identity is louder than others, and in what moments might that take place?

Addressing Model	Agent	Target
Age & Generational Influences	18–65	Younger than 18; older than 65
Developmental Disabilities	IQ above 70; no learning issues	IQ under 70; compromised learning; developmental delays
Disability (acquired or congenital, physical, cognitive, psychological, visible, invisible disabilities)	Able in all areas	Disabilities from injuries, illnesses, trauma
Dogma (beliefs, philosophy, politics)	Supported by current social values	Different from current social values
Religion and Spiritual Orientation	Christianity, Christian values, Christian celebrating; no religious preference	Jewish; Muslim; all non-Christian practices
Race (self-identified): uni-, bi-, multiracial	White	Black; indigenous; People of Color; biracial; multiracial
Region (rural, urban, suburban, exurban)	Urban, suburban, exurban (depends on client's location)	Rural (depends on client's location)
Relationship status	Coupled	Single; legally unrecognized relationships; polyamory
Ethnicity: uni-, bi-, and multiethnic	Euro-Americans; white	Non Euro-American; unrecognized ethnicities (i.e., those that have faced genocide, loss of identity, etc.)
Socioeconomic status (class)	Middle and high SES	Poverty and low SES; financial dependence; lack of financial support
Sexual orientation	Heterosexual, straight	Lesbian; gay; bisexual; asexual; pansexual
Size	Socially sanctioned weight	Not socially sanctioned weight
Indigenous Heritage	Non-native	Native, indigenous; unrecognized, other
Incarceration	Never incarcerated	Incarcerated
National Origin	Born in the United States; United States citizen	Voluntary/involuntary immigration; undocumented; colonial state refugee
Neurodiversity	Neurotypical	Twice exceptionality; overexcitability
Gender	Cisgender men	Women; transgender; intersex Two spirit; People assigned female at birth; Nonbinary; gender-fluid; agender; genderqueer; gender nonconforming
Genetics	Biologically related to parents	Adopted; fostered; stepchild
Trauma	No traumatic experiences	Experience of traumatic events; estrangement; disownment; incarceration

Adapted from Pamela A. Hays, "Resilience and the ADDRESSING Model," *Addressing Cultural Complexities in Practice: A Framework for Clinicians and Counselors.* Copyright © 2001 by American Psychological Association.

Terms

Agent	People and groups who have initiative, power, and privilege.
Target	People and groups who are oppressed and marginalized.

Clinician's Profile

	A	D	D	d	R	r	r	r	E	S	S	I	N	G	g	g	t
Agent																	
Target																	

Adapted from Hays, 2001

_____

_____

_____

_____

_____

_____

References

Hays, P. (2001). *Addressing cultural complexities in practice*. American Psychological Association.

Unpacking Your Privilege

Intention

When we enter a therapeutic relationship, it is unrealistic to think we can check our intersectionalities, beliefs, values, assumptions, bias, and privileges at the door. If we choose to ignore these aspects of ourselves, we may unintentionally cause harm to our clients. Engaging in challenging difficult conversations with ourselves may elicit an open space to broach these subjects with our clients.

Written Reflection

| Duration: 10 minutes | Materials Needed: Pen/Paper |

Refer back to the Resilience and the ADDRESSING Model invitation and list your privileged identities. Consider the following:

- How might you deconstruct reactive biases and create awareness around your privilege?
- What assumptions do you make of others who may not hold these privileges?
- What stories do you hold around these privileges that perpetuate oppressive narratives?

_____

_____

_____

_____

_____

_____

Somatic Invitation

Duration: 10 minutes | Materials Needed: None

Take a moment to embody privilege and a sense of power over someone else, playing with a sense of tension in the upper body. Perhaps this is a tightening around the face/eyes, a judgmental or critical mindset. This could also look like experimenting with inhabiting the posture of your concept of a villain.

Where does this sense of power live within you? Does it feel soft/hard? Easy to carry? Does it bring up other sensations or feelings? Does it feel familiar or foreign?

_____

_____

_____

_____

_____

_____

Decolonizing Systems

Intention

As mentioned with the "Throwing out the Toolbox" invitation, we learn a lot about the history of evidence-based theories as counselors-in-training. Within this history, learning about the systemic underpinnings and history of theory development is important, including sociopolitical, historical, and personal influences that formed the theories. These theories are centered around westernized, White voices, which can highlight sociopolitical roles based on white supremacy and classism, perpetuate privilege, and exclude populations.

Verbal/Written Reflection

Duration: 10–30 minutes   Materials Needed: Pen/Paper, Partner/Group

Decolonizing Theory

Consider a theory that you are interested in learning more about or even utilizing in your future practice as a counselor, and reflect on the following:

- Who developed the theory?
- What intersecting privileges do they hold?
- What was happening in their family system during their own development? How might this inform the way they thought about human personality, development, and how individuals think and move through the world?
- What was the political climate during this time?
- What aspects of the theory do you think need to be decolonized?

Case Study

In a group or dyad, read the following case study and consider the following questions:

- What multicultural and social justice issues could arise with the therapist's approach with Elena?
- What does the therapist need to consider when working with Elena?

The client, Elena, is a 28-year-old Latina cis-female individual. She mentioned that she is primarily coming to therapy because she is struggling to connect with others and have a social life outside of her family members, with whom she is really close. She also mentioned that she feels some stress trying to "make ends meet" while working paycheck to paycheck. Her therapist is a white male who typically uses person-centered therapy with his clients. He reflected to Elena that when thinking about her needs, it may be hard to feel connected to others while she is worried about paying for rent, food, and other living expenses.

Engaging in these conversations, creating awareness for yourself as you utilize these theories with your clients, and staying curious and open to their experiences is a starting point to decolonizing counseling systems.

CHAPTER 9

RESILIENCE-CENTERED RELATIONSHIPS

1. THE MIRACLE QUESTION FOR COUNSELORS
2. FOCUSING ON CONNECTION

The Miracle Question for Counselors

Intention

Milton Erickson (1954) asked clients to describe how they were able to solve their problems upon meeting their therapist at some time in the future. He called this the "pseudo-orientation in time" technique and provided a shift in working with the end in mind. Steve de Shazer (1985) paralleled this idea through the use of a "miracle question" that encouraged clients to imagine a life when the problem was solved and "more on track." Each quickly shifted the frame (perspective) in order to open up possibilities. Steve de Shazer incorporated this into a social constructivist paradigm and used this as a way to quickly shift the conversation away from problem talk (that was just a recursive narrative loop) toward the co-construction of possibility between the counselor and client—thus exiting the deficit loop into something preferred. The elegance of the miracle question was not in the question itself, but with the counselor's ability to encourage clients to keep looking forward toward perceived competence rather than backward toward helplessness.

Written Reflection

Duration: 5–10 minutes	Materials Needed: Pen/Paper

Below is a miracle question for counselors. It is designed to shift away from seeing clients as victims of their history and prisoners to their symptoms and toward an envisioned stance of experiencing them as capable and resilient. Please reflect on this with pen in hand and note how this influences what you notice in your next client session.

For a moment, consider a current client and how you experience them. Now imagine that a miracle occurs between now and the next time the two of you meet. In this miracle, you see only the possible in the client. You have an absolute and unquestionable belief in the capability and inner resources of the client. Although hidden previously, in this miracle, all you can see in this client are their undeniable strengths and their efforts in keeping their head above water. You are concerned only with who they are becoming and can't help but notice the virtues and values that they have often sacrificed in efforts to reduce their suffering. Finally, in this miracle, you notice only what is right with the client and how you have been impacted by your work with them. A sense of gratitude and humility are far more present in your experience as the miracle of the next session unfolds.

- Hold this miracle close and imagine how this would inform how you show up to the next session. How would you experience the client?
- How would they experience you?

- What would be different about you?
- What would be different about your intent and clinical focus?
- How might this perspective influence your work with others and with yourself?
- What would be the first sign in your work with others that this miracle is beginning to take hold—even just a little bit?

Somatic Invitation

Duration: 10 minutes   Materials Needed: None

Think about the answer to your own miracle question or the miracle scenario above. Spend some time embodying what this might feel like. Consider acting it out with a partner, using dancing, singing, or any other form of expression that you feel connected to.

Is this embodiment joyous? Is it jumpy? What is it like to embody this miracle and incorporate it into your own physical energy?

References

De Shazer, S. (1985). *Keys to solution in brief therapy* (1st ed., Ser. A Norton professional book). W. W. Norton.

Erickson, M. H. (1954). Special techniques of brief hypnotherapy. *Journal of Clinical and Experimental Hypnosis*, *2*(2), 109–129. https://doi.org/10.1080/00207145408409943

Focusing on Connection

Intention

Resilience can be a westernized construct that focuses on the individual rather than systems and community. The focus on many theories can be on individualistic thinking rather than considering macro and meso systems that affect a person's life (like religion, community, socioeconomic status, gender, race, oppression, marginalization). Additionally, this individualistic focus in itself marginalizes large groups of people considering that the world is at least 70% collectivist. When there is an individualized focus, there is not a lot of space to consider cultures that focus on family/community and make decisions through that lens. This activity will challenge you to consider thinking of the community, connection, and relational aspects of counseling.

Written/Verbal Reflection

Duration: 5–10 minutes	Materials Needed: Pen/Paper, Partner optional

Identifying Community

Did you know that just one aspen tree is actually a small part of a larger organism? If you see a group of aspen trees, you are really looking at a singular organism with the "main life force underground in the extensive root system" (Featherman, n.d.). Similar to the aspen tree network is the growth of mycelium from mushrooms that creates an underground network where all living things communicate and support one another (Schwartzberg, 2019).

Think about the trees or mycelium in your own life and consider the following questions:

- Who are your support systems?
- What is communication like within this system?
- What do your supports say to you in a time of need?

Sharing in Community

In a dyad, discuss a moment where you experienced frustration, irritation, sadness, or anger. Process together what it is like to share in these experiences. Share your experience of having felt a sense of resilience with your dyad partner.

Imagery Exploration

Duration: 10+ minutes   Materials Needed: Multimedia

Draw your tree/mycelium network using any medium that you may feel connected to at this moment. Feel free to express as much information as you feel comfortable with. Use the above reflective questions in the written/verbal reflection above to think about how you want to portray these pieces of your network/community.

References

Featherman, Hannah (n.d.) Tree Profile: Aspen—so much more than a tree. *National Forest Foundation*. https://www.nationalforests.org/blog/tree-profile-aspen-so-much-more-than-a-tree

Schwartzberg, L. (Director). (2019). *Fantastic Fungi* [Documentary]. Moving Art Studio.

CHAPTER 10

A RESILIENT SOCIAL JUSTICE STANCE

Missed Opportunities

Intention

The text highlights that when we put blinders on our own beliefs and ideas, we can miss the unique stories of others' lived experiences; we miss connecting with others. Additionally, we impact others when we listen with judgment compared to when we listen with humility and compassion. Regardless of our inherent skill set, listening is a skill that requires intention and thoughtfulness.

Verbal/Written Reflection

Duration: 5–10 minutes	Materials Needed: Pen/Paper optional

Reflect on a moment when you were sharing an experience with someone and you felt like they were not hearing you or did not understand where you were coming from. Process what feelings come up for you around this. What did it feel like to be not understood? What would it have looked like for the other person to listen with intention?

Now think about a situation in which you were the individual listening and not understanding another's unique experience. What blocked you from listening, being open, and learning about this person's experience? How might your own judgment have been in the way of hearing their story?

Imagery Exploration

Duration: 10–15 minutes | Materials Needed: Pen/Paper

The countertransference process is relational and requires counselors to hold the duality of connection and difference between themselves and their client and have awareness of the middle ground.

Reflect back to the "Telling Stories: Invitations for Collaborative Change" imagery exploration and the visual representation of a net on page 29.

Think about the "common threads" that you may share with a particular client.

Take a piece of paper and draw a line from left to right on the page for each common thread that you have identified with your client. Then, draw a line from the top of the page to the bottom for each way that you are different from your client, representing "uncommon threads."

Once again, consider this visual representation as a net of the therapeutic relationship. What do you notice about the threads and the importance of their existence? Perhaps, rather than thinking about either/or, consider that the net needs both the commonalities and differences in order to hold the relationship.

Mapping It Out

Intention

When we share a space with a client, it is important to recognize the intersectionality of our clients as well as ourselves and also understand our autonomic nervous system functioning. The Person of the Therapist Training Model (POTT) was developed by Harry Aponte to offer space for clinicians to bring themselves to the therapeutic process while also processing personal and emotional aspects that may interfere with their clinical effectiveness (Aponte & Carlsen, 2009). Watson (1993) clearly articulated that person of the therapist is paramount to the therapeutic relationship because the therapist is not excluded from the relationship and therefore needs self-awareness and reflection. The POTT model emphasizes the therapist knowing themself, observing and accessing countertransference, managing oneself in the therapeutic space, and identifying and differentiating self from the client (Aponte et al., 2009). Essentially, we must know ourselves, including our culture, values, beliefs, and how we show up and impact the therapeutic relationship.

Written Reflection

Duration: 20+ minutes	Materials Needed: Pen/Paper, Multimedia

Genogram Creation

Part of the POTT process consists of drawing a three-generational family genogram and processing the relational dynamics, intergenerational patterns and themes that you notice from your family system (adapted from Bean et al., 2014). How do these themes show up in your current values and beliefs? What aspects of your family system inform how you may be in a relationship with your clients? Take some time to reflect on these questions and other takeaways you have from this experience and share them with your supervisor or dyad partner.

For help to get started on your genogram see the following website: https://genopro.com/articles/how-to-create-a-genogram/

Understanding the Autonomic Nervous System (ANS)

Connecting our values and beliefs to our own neurobiological responses:

Grab a piece of paper and divide it into three columns. In the far left column, write out some personal sympathetic nervous system (SNS) responses that you experience. In the far right column, write out personal parasympathetic nervous system (PNS) responses. These responses can be reflective of both individual and relational experiences or events. In the middle column, consider what things help regulate your ANS that move you from the SNS/hot feelings to the PNS/cool feelings.

Now consider this process when someone has offered you companionship alongside a deep and intense emotional experience. How might this impact your regulation? What information might this give you with how you may hold space for a client in a highly dysregulated state?

_____

_____

_____

_____

_____

Imagery Exploration

Duration: 20+ minutes   Materials Needed: Multimedia

The following invitation was created by Dr. Katherine Fort at Antioch University, Seattle, while teaching a multicultural supervision course to counselor education and supervision doctoral candidates in the third quarter of their program. See Appendix A for insight into this invitation from the perspective of the students who engaged in this imagery exploration.

Imagine your intersectionality. Think of your values, beliefs, family values, attributes or characteristics, and roles that make up who you are. Create a visual representation of your cocultures and intersectionalities. The Jones and McEwen (2000) Model of Multiple Dimensions may be used as a starting point for engaging in this activity. For example, you may think about your family background, sociocultural conditions, current experiences, personal attributes, characteristics, and identity and how these pieces of self interconnect. How might you best depict your intersectionality? Feel free to use what medium(s) you are drawn to (paper/pencil, painting/drawing, etc.) in order to express yourself in a way that feels congruent to you. If you are comfortable sharing, do so with a partner, friend, supervisor, etc.

_____

_____

_____

_____

References

Aponte, H. J., & Carlsen, J. C. (2009, September 25). An instrument for person-of-the-therapist supervision. *Journal of Marital and Family Therapy, 35*(4), 395–405. https://doi.org/10.1111/j.1752-0606.2009.00127.x

Aponte, H. J., Powell, F. D., Brooks, S., Watson, M. F., Litzke, C., Lawless, J., & Johnson, E. (2009). Training the person of the therapist in an academic setting. *Journal of Marital and Family Therapy, 35*(4), 381–94. https://doi.org/10.1111/j.1752-0606.2009.00123.x

Bean, R., Davis, S., & Davey, M. (2014). *Clinical supervision activities for increasing competence and self-awareness.* Wiley, Inc.

Jones, S. R., & McEwen, M. K. (2000). A conceptual model of multiple dimensions of identity. *Journal of College Student Development, 41*(4), 405–14.

Watson, M. F. (1993). Supervising the person of the therapist: issues, challenges and dilemmas. *Contemporary Family Therapy, 15*(1), 21–31. https://doi.org/10.1007/BF00903485

Myths of Meritocracy

Intention

There is a notion in westernized, individualized culture that "anyone can do that," and it perpetuates the harmful bootstrap theory. Within this notion is the idea that everyone has access to or is supported equally within the system, which is simply a fallacy. As counselors, we can fuel this problematic thinking by conceptualizing clients only through diagnosis and treatment, rather than considering the systemic factors that impact their unique experiences. Once again, this process of dismantling starts with unpacking and understanding our own lived experiences, values, and beliefs.

Verbal/Written Reflection

Duration: 5–15 minutes   Materials Needed: Pen/Paper

Reflect back on the imagery exploration in the "Mapping It Out" invitation on page 54. Choose three identities you named for yourself and consider the following:

1. Describe the value system that may be attached to each identity and its context of culture.
2. How does this value system impact the way you see others?
3. Consider a client whose values are different from yours. What are your automatic thoughts regarding this client?
4. Consider how you might have a dialogue with this client about their values and perspectives, rather than jumping to a biased conclusion.

Example: Elliot, a counselor, sees themself as an educator and values education. This value leaves space for Elliot to create assumptions about a client who may not have finished high school. It impacts how he conceptualizes this client and leaves room for bias to arise.

_____

_____

_____

_____

Imagery Exploration

Duration: 5–10 minutes   Materials Needed: Pen/Paper

Take a moment to refer back to your genogram from the verbal/written reflection in the "Mapping It Out" invitation. Reflect on the following:

- What individual or individuals in your family hold similar values to you—values that you find most important to your identity? Name the individual(s) and values.
- What are some biases attached to these values?

CHAPTER 11

SURFING

1.   INOCULATION

Inoculation

Intention

Inoculation is a reflective experience to stimulate an intentional neurobiological response in the face of stress-inducing situations.

Somatic Invitation and Written Reflection

Duration: 10–15 minutes	Materials Needed: Pen/Paper optional

The steps below are designed to increase self-confidence, highlighting an invitation to one's "best self" in resistance to anxious and worrisome thoughts. The development of a mindset empowers one to be in greater service to a set of personal strengths and values, rather than in reaction to stress-producing situations or interactions.

Step One: Grounding

- Bring attention to your breathing. It can open space in recognition of the moment, and, as this occurs, pay attention to any thoughts or images that arise. Be attuned to the idea of "letting go and letting in."
- Briefly notice the relaxing sensation of air traveling back and forth though your nasal passage and how this allows other parts of your body to relax (e.g., shoulders).

Step Two: Witnessing

- Imagine a situation where you wish a greater sense of freedom in your response to worry, anxiety, and/or fear. Witness in your mind's eye the impact that this trigger situation has on your experience:
  - what you feel (physical tension/sensations)
  - how you feel (emotional responses)
  - images and thoughts weaving in and out (self-narrative)
- Be sure to pause before your thoughts/feelings escalate to the "worst scenario."

Step Three: Holding

- Imagine your better self:
  - Imagine what you would like to remember about yourself. What strengths will you apply (e.g., openness, optimism, honesty) that will be more in service to your personal values (e.g., kindness, compassion, contribution)?
  - What compassion for yourself would help to keep your anxious thoughts at bay? What do you notice (ideas, feelings, sensations) as irritation and worry that have less of a hold on you? What wisdom does this carry for you?
- Imagine your better relationships:
  - How can you remember that the best way to reduce interpersonal conflict is to hold space for multiple perspectives, rather than only your own—which can lead to blame and resentment?
  - Express what is true for you and allow the other to do the same.

Step Four: Reflect

- Focus on slowing and reflecting on the mindset as noted above. Imagine being more in service to this mindset than in reaction to the situation or others.
- Resist the impulse to blame (the other or yourself). Stay open to diverse perspectives as you reflect on staying conscious of your best self.

Step Five: Apply

- Ground, witness, hold, and reflect as much as possible during the week. This can be done in quiet contemplation or in movement (e.g., walking, hiking, listening to music, and/or performing other creative activities). To remember the better parts of ourselves is to inoculate present and future stress-inducing situations. This is the foundation for resilient living.
- Notice situations where you feel the pull of self-protection, as well as opportunities to apply a mindset that allows for increased degrees of personal and professional confidence.
- Identify small ways to apply this mindset at work and at home. Take note (without self-judgment) of actions and attitudes that might need revising.
- Finally, employ the power of mind–body medicine by pausing and reflecting on how our better selves can be more present in stressful situations. We become what we predict. To inoculate oneself against the neurobiological reaction to high levels of anxiety and fear is to bring increased access to executive brain function: an intentional response in service to a preferred mindset rather than in reaction to a protective stress response (flight, fight, and freeze).

CHAPTER 12

WONDERMENT

A Resilient Centered Approach for Deconstructing Narratives

Intention

Shared understanding between clients and counselors becomes less about the story itself and more about how the story defines the storyteller—an attunement to what is being experienced of what is being said.

Verbal/Written Reflection

Duration: 5–15 minutes	Materials Needed: Pen/Paper

The following sets of questions are designed to develop a case narrative illustrating the client experience in counseling. The focus questions can be used to broaden the counselor's perception of client experiences or shared with clients to assist with broadening their perception of themselves.

Struggle Perception

- Describe the client's perception of their hurt. What might they call it? What is the client's theory about how the hurt developed and why change has proven difficult?
- What impact is this having on them? In what ways does the "long arm of the past" take hold of the client?
- Describe the emotional impact this struggle with hurt is having on them? What does the hurt secretly whisper in the ear of the client?
- In what ways is the client attached to the hurt? What would be compromised if the client decided to think or act differently to the hurt?
- What is the hurt/trauma event robbing from them? What is being sacrificed? What personal hopes are being dashed or diminished?

Resilient Efforts

- What is sustaining them in the face of their struggle with hurt? Describe the "rest of the client story" about how they keep hurt from "taking over."
- How would you describe the client's better self? In what ways is their better self compromised in the context of their struggle?

- Describe the client in reference to the 4 C's of resilience:
  - connection to a caring support network;
  - cultural identity of shared experiences, beliefs, and values;
  - community engagement and service to values beyond the self; and
  - capacity for tolerating dissonance, ambiguity, and multiplicity.
- Imagine a time in the future when you and the client meet:
  - What will they be sharing about what they learned? About others and relationships? About their hopes for the future?
  - If you were to believe this to be true for the client, even just a little bit, how might that change your interaction with them?

Stretching

Intention

Stretching, growing, expanding, evolving. These words may activate discomfort, or perhaps pain in some of us, because they mean that a shift or change is occurring. As counselors, it's important to understand how we have been stretched by life's adversities and to explore this relationally with our clients.

Somatic Invitation

Duration: 10–15 minutes	Materials Needed: None, Multimedia optional

Mary Starks Whitehouse began movement-in-depth in the 1950s to explore the mind–body–spirit connection through dance and movement (Hendricks, 2010). Today it is better known as Authentic Movement Therapy.

Find a space that is comfortable for free movement. While staying present and with your eyes closed, think about your inner emotions. Take your time to begin moving your body, perhaps swaying back and forth or stretching. When you feel ready, begin moving your body through the experience of your emotions in whatever way feels right and connected to you and for whatever duration of time you need.

When you are ready, take a moment to reflect on this physical act of stretching and moving. Perhaps process where this felt comfortable or difficult. Sit with and strive to appreciate the multiplicity of emotions and experiences this movement allows. Feel free to write down your thoughts, draw, color, or reflect in ways that may be helpful to you.

_____

_____

_____

_____

_____

Verbal Reflection

Duration: 10–15 minutes   Materials Needed: Pen/Paper

In a dyad, share a story about when you were stretching, growing, evolving, etc. As the listener, challenge yourself to focus less on the story your partner is sharing and simply use both/and reflections back to them. Once both partners have shared and listened, process with one another what this experience was like. Plan to spend about 5 minutes in each role.

_____

_____

_____

_____

References

Hendricks, K. T. (2010). What I learned from Mary: Reflections on the work of Mary Starks Whitehouse. *American Journal of Dance Therapy : Publication of the American Dance Therapy Association*, *32*(1), 64–68. https://doi.org/10.1007/s10465-009-9073-3

Being in Becoming

Intention

Becoming. Regardless of the context, becoming is a process that takes time and evolves as our perceptions of self shift and as we interpret new experiences and their meaning toward growth. The process of becoming is omnipresent; it is important to take time, slow down, and reflect on previous and current stories of becoming.

Verbal/Written Reflection

Duration: 5–10+ minutes	Materials Needed: Pen/Paper or Partner/Group

In a dyad or group or writing individually, share a story of your own becoming—whether past or present. Examples include becoming a student, parent, teacher, colleague, counselor, etc. Reflect on the following:

- What did you notice about your narrative?
- Has the way that you told this story changed over the course of becoming?
- What was it like to share this story?
- What did you learn about yourself as you were growing into this particular role?

Somatic Invitation

Duration: 5–10 minutes   Materials Needed: None

Think about the developmental process and narrative of becoming that you explored above. Spend some time acting out your story or journey of getting to where you are now. Consider acting it out, dancing, or moving your body in a way that connects to your narrative. Think about the ways each phase of becoming shows up in your movements—beginning, intermediate, present. What is your body telling you about this narrative? How does your body shift through each of these phases?

CHAPTER 13

STRENGTHENING

Cultural Strengthening

Intention

In collectivist cultures, resilience is manifested relationally (Leake & Black, 2005) and highlights how service, a commitment to one's community, reflects the interdependent bond between others and the importance of connection. Resilience is far more than an emphasis on self-reliance and autonomy; instead, it develops through shared experiences that help modulate dysregulating emotions and provide a container for holding silence without fear and connection over protection.

Verbal/Written Reflection

Duration: 10–15 minutes	Materials Needed: Pen/Paper, Partner optional

With pen in hand, and referencing the chart on page 39 of the text, reflect on the following questions:

- What aspects of your cultural experience might be influencing how you are holding your current struggle? What would be expected of you from a cultural perspective?
- Who held the cultural voice in your family? In what ways does this influence you today?
- Consider the moment when you were at your best (or closer to it). What strengths were you tapping into that seemed to give rise to your best self?
- How do you balance the values that are important to you today with cultural and family expectations?
- When you are closer to your best in reference to your gender, orientation, race, etc., what might this say about what is important to you ... and what you might be learning about yourself?

Write these reflections in a journal or discuss them with a learning partner and consider how your reactions represent your cultural experiences as well as the quality of your relationships.

References

Leake, D., & Black, R. (2005). Cultural and linguistic diversity: Implications for transition personnel. Essential tools: improving secondary education and transition for youth with disabilities. ERIC Clearinghouse.

Remembering Our Better Self

Intention

The questions below are an invitation to one's "best self" in resistance to anxious and worrisome thoughts. The best self can promote a mindset that empowers one to be in greater service to a set of personal strengths and values, rather than in reaction to stress-producing situations or interactions. In many ways we become what we can predict. To inoculate oneself against the neurobiological reaction to high levels of anxiety and fear is to bring increased access to executive brain function: an intentional response in service to a preferred mindset rather than in reaction to a protective stress response (flight, fight, and freeze).

Verbal/Written Reflection

Duration: 10–15 minutes	Materials Needed: Pen/Paper, Partner optional

With a partner, consider a recent moment when you were closer to your better self and discuss the questions below. (If it is not possible to do the exercise with a partner, this can be completed with pen in hand.) Seek to do so without interpretation, only remembering those times that represented more of who you seek to be more often (even if the occasions were not perfect). Paint a picture in your mind's eye upon completion, and note any physical or emotional sensations.

- What was different about you in that moment from other life moments?
- What feelings were more alive in you?
- What strengths might you have been tapping into that seemed to give rise to your better self?
- What values were you holding close? What seemed at the forefront of your mind?
- What was alive in you that others might have witnessed during this moment in time? What did they receive from you and you from them?

_____

_____

_____

_____

Strengthening Requires Sacrifice

Intention

Empirical models often seek to replace the known (e.g., symptoms of worry, anxiety, and depression) with thoughts and actions that are unknown and foreign. A client's unwillingness to step into the deep abyss of fear and uncertainty to the untried and unknown is often interpreted as resistance by well-meaning clinicians. It highlights a binary view where health is represented by the absence of the problem or symptoms and tantamount to asking people with a fear of water to swim by jumping into the deep end of the pool. Hesitancy and fear would be natural reactions when invited to try something both new and dangerous—a danger often imperceptible from those privileged with the skills and confidence for swimming. Resilient centered clinicians consider not just the desired outcomes as expressed by clients, but the experience of what it might take, and the sacrifice required, in order to begin.

Written Reflection

Duration: 5–10 minutes   Materials Needed: Pen/Paper

Consider someone in your life (client, colleague, friend, yourself) that is in the midst of a struggle. Imagine their struggle as experienced by them, and reflect on the questions below:

- What are they sacrificing that keeps the struggle alive?
- What is the struggle robbing them of?
- What might the absence of the struggle mean for them, both in terms of personal freedoms and profound loss?

_____

_____

_____

_____

Somatic Invitation

Duration: 10–20 minutes	Materials Needed: Partner

In a dyad, each person will take turns telling a story of a struggle they experienced. As the listener, experiment with embodying or mirroring the posture of the storyteller. Spend about 3 to 5 minutes in each role.

As the listener/embodier, what sensations came alive for you while you were embodying your partner?

As the storyteller, what was it like to see your posture mirrored back to you as you were sharing your struggle?

_____

_____

_____

_____

_____

Defining Strength

Intention

As stated in the introduction, language is important and there is not only one definition for the terminology used throughout this workbook. Defining a concept for yourself is part of the process of understanding and learning what automatic thoughts arise for you when a client uses a similar concept; it is a way to be aware and stay intentionally curious.

Written Reflection

Duration: 5–10 minutes   Materials Needed: Pen/Paper

In order to unpack your own cultural views of strength, reflect and write on the following questions:

- How do you define strength?
- What does it look like to be strong?
- What does it feel like to be strong?
- Is this concept individual, collective, or both?
- How did you learn what strength is?

_____

_____

_____

_____

_____

Somatic Invitation

Duration: 5–10 minutes   Materials Needed: None or Partner/Group optional

Take a moment to get into a comfortable standing position. Begin shifting your weight back and forth, forward and backward between your feet. When you have found equal weight distribution across the bottoms of your feet, imagine that with each inhalation roots are growing outward and more deeply into the earth. Imagine that with each exhalation, branches are reaching toward the sky as you invite openness and expansion across your chest. How does this grounded and openness relate to your strength?

If working in a dyad or group, imagine your roots and branches interconnecting with each other. What feels differently for you when you are connected? How does this inform your strength narrative?

_____

_____

_____

_____

_____

_____

Mapping It Out Imagery Exploration: Student Reflections

My representation included the following items: (a) a black and white photo of my paternal grandmother; (b) a picture of me and my partner in a hot spring in Idaho; (c) a repurposed pillow made from my mother's old mink coat; (d) a piece of dried coral with many holes; (e) a surgical mask; (f) a wooden giraffe doing a yoga pose; (g) a kaleidoscope; (h) a metal frog doing another yoga pose; and (i) in the center, an abstract watercolor depiction of the multiple facets of my identity.

The experience for me was incredibly powerful. I was able to share pieces of myself with my cohort members that felt vulnerable and authentic. At one point, I got surprisingly emotional with feelings of sadness, longing, complexity, confusion, and vulnerability dancing together in my inner world. No longer able or wanting to keep those to myself, sharing them through story, image, and objects facilitated a sense of groundedness to my own truth and sense of the world. Feeling the support and connection to my peers allowed an embodiment of learning that has continued to percolate into my present experiences as a student, supervisor, and educator.

Overall, I really appreciated the freedom of this assignment to utilize different formats. I think this freedom and novelty nurtured my ability to recall my cohort mate's projects as well. Absorbing their presentations allowed me to see them in their deeper layers of complexity and intersectionalities. Engaging in creativity brought in a sense of spirituality, playfulness, and fun. For me, these aspects fostered our relationships with one another as a learning community in an invaluable way.

—Laura Durkin, MA, LMFT

IMG 2

Before I started on my artwork, I did a spiritual/mental cleansing type process to help me get into a creative mood. I did an activity based on the five senses: smell, touch, taste, hearing, and sight. I also did some meditation to clear my mind of all the things I had on my mind. I also watched Buddhist monks at Clark College in Vancouver, Washington, create a mandala from sand art called "The Buddha of Compassion." I performed these activities to help me gain access to my creative mind, so to speak. I decided to create a mandala, which was based on my intersectionality. I have created a mandala in the past, during undergrad for my personality theories psychology class.

Creating a mandala is a sacred and spiritual journey and experience. While creating my mandala this time around, I immediately fell into a trancelike state as I began to pick out my layout, colored pencils, and the rest of the art supplies that I needed. The rest of the world completely fell away. It was as if no one in the world existed except for myself and the spirit of creativity that consumed me. It was as if nothing mattered or existed for that moment in time. My mandala is a partial circle, which represents room for growth mentally, spiritually, physically, and professionally. When the circle becomes complete, that will mean to me that I have achieved an impermanence state of being, old age. And it will mean that I have learned many things and that I will continue to change and grow, until the very end.

—Akimma Wright-D'Abreau, LSWAIC, MHP

I came into counseling in midlife. It is my third career. The traumas that I experienced as a child, adolescent, and young adult feel distant. I know they are still there, but they don't arise as sucker punch energies any longer. These traumas are of the type from which made-for-TV movies are written. They are the wells from which 1990s daytime talk show hosts drew their stories. These traumas have color.

When I was younger, I sometimes shared these stories, mostly with strangers, thrilling in the attention of their shock. My outward presentation—polished, put-together, pretty—was no match for their expectation of someone who had lived through such a life. I would smile in their confusion as they took in the lurid details I passed out like candy. I wore my scars on my sleeve and sometimes let them glint in the sunlight, then gloried in the flash when others repulsed at the ugly.

As the decades slipped past, though, I have tempered, softened, pulled within, and I have found much greater strength in not telling. Strangers need not know. The stories slipped down, became dull, faded to earth tones as they integrated into my past, not the present. Not even my now-closest friends have ever heard what happened when I was young.

As part of my training to become a counselor, I of course was requested to do so much self-reflection—which is important, and so useful, in the process of becoming a therapist who can listen and hear. An active practice of self-inquiry is a significant reason I have found so much peace in these years. But share such disclosures with others? Reveal who I actually am? No. All papers I wrote for school were carefully scrubbed. Black-and-white only, no color, no need to brush off the dirt down below. I was proud to say that I had survived much, while skipping what was survived.

Until quite recently, I would have labeled these preferences for personal privacy as resilience—that my traumas form the undergirding of my strength, and my strategies to keep those stories to myself make me ever stronger. I believed that being reserved was protective, and my personal story is best kept only for me. I believed this fully and completely—until there was suddenly a tap on that hard candy shell.

The main character of a long-ago trauma story has reentered the scene of my life, 30 years later, and I have been forced to reexamine all assumptions. This disruption of my carefully-tended normalcy has shown me the traumas are still there and active. They were not as deeply buried as I thought. I am rattled by what has transpired—so rattled I pulled out the DSM and looked at my old friend PTSD.

So what is resilience? Is it coping in the face of a new stressor? For me, resilience means I have the ability to now choose differently. I am absolutely reliving these dead-buried traumas again in this modern-day moment, and my resilience is telling me I can face it. I am finding myself ready—this time—to seek connection. I am telling my story. I am doing it here, in code and anonymously, but I am doing it.

My resilience this time will be found through letting others inside, to let them see the ugly with me, and help me to bear it.

—Anonymous

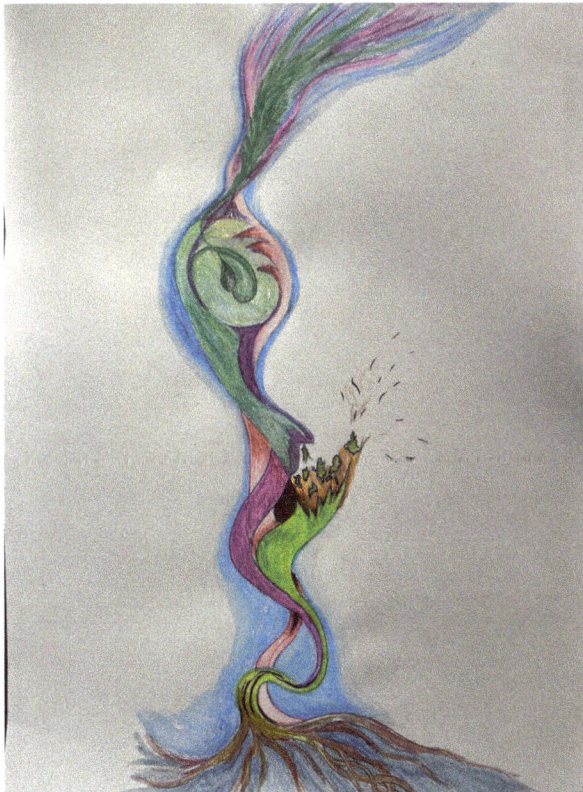

I have come to understand that working on the person of the therapist is such an important part of nurturing our ongoing identity, but also something that can really get lost in the day-to-day work of being a therapist. The CES supervision course provided an exciting challenge in the opportunity to really explore questions such as the following: Who am I? Who have I been? What signature theme or themes have run through my life? It required me to dig back into previous versions of myself, some of which were painful and not pretty.

I think a pathway into my reflective process really opened up when our professor encouraged us to think outside the academic box in our method of responding to the prompt in order to stretch ourselves emotionally and intellectually. I chose to complete the project using art (see attached). As I thought about the themes of marriage, family, trauma, health, and professional identity, I was able to represent how these life threads have woven together, interacting and influencing one another. As I worked to represent the interwoven themes artistically, I also found myself integrating who I am now with parts of myself that I once wanted to just leave behind. I was able to see the beauty in the struggles I have experienced and the growth that has occurred from those struggles.

—Jennifer S. Kennett, MA, LHMC

IMG 5

In order to explore my intersectionalities, I decided to engage in a sand tray activity that allowed me to express how my identity connects with others. One of the biggest areas of my identity is culture, as it connects with several other aspects of how I identify myself. My identification as a Latina intersects with my gender, religion, education, languages, classes, sexual orientation, and occupation. Using the sand tray allowed me to connect with my intersectionalities in a deeper and more meaningful way than just writing a reflection.

—Gladys Lopez, MA, LPCC

ADDITIONAL NOTES

ADDITIONAL NOTES

ADDITIONAL NOTES